NATIONAL GEOGRAPHIC

Ladders

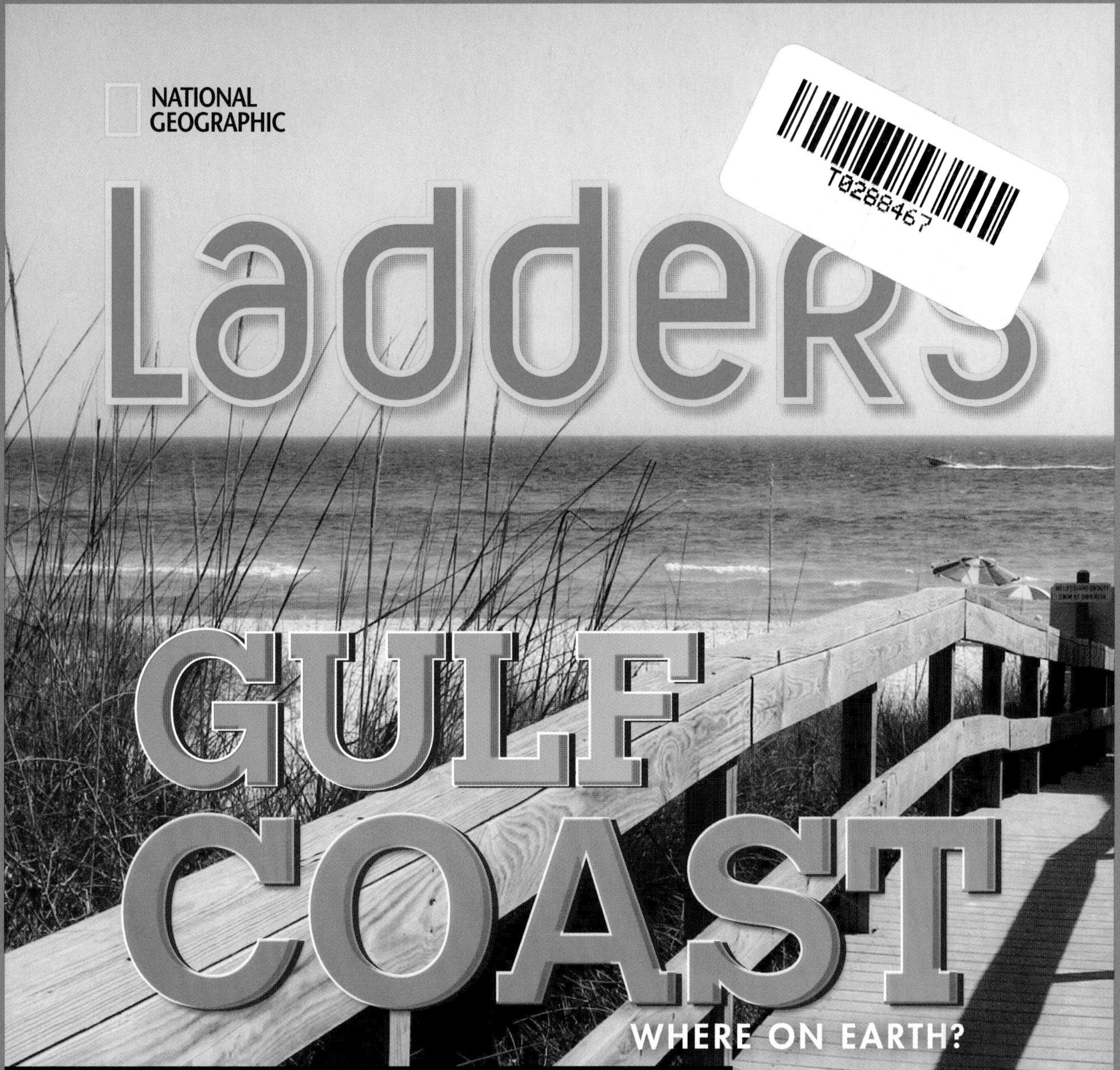

GULF COAST

WHERE ON EARTH?

GENRE **Social Studies Article**

Read to find out about the geography and wildlife of the Gulf Coast.

Welcome to the Gulf Coast

by Sherri Patoka

You're standing on a warm, sunny beach watching the waves splash toward you. Sand oozes between your toes. Water from the Gulf of Mexico races toward the shore and flows through tall grass. The regular flooding of the tide over the grass creates a **tidal marsh**. Tidal marshes make up a large part of this coastal region, and provide a home for many plants and animals.

This lush region is called the Gulf Coast of the United States. It's located along the Gulf of Mexico, a large body of water that's connected to the Atlantic Ocean. The Gulf lies between the United States and Mexico. It is almost entirely surrounded by land. Because of this, its water doesn't move as much as the open ocean, so it gets really salty.

The swampy, marshy parts of the Gulf Coast host all kinds of animals, including alligators, turtles, and wading birds. Twisty, tangled trees called **mangroves** grow in the hot, wet environment.

The land near the coast isn't only swamp, though. As you wander away from the ocean, the wet grassy marsh turns into beaches and hilly sand **dunes**. People who like being near the sea and hot, sunny weather live along the Gulf Coast.

This Gulf Coast beach is in Baldwin County, Alabama.

Where on Earth?

THE GULF COAST

There are lots of places to explore on the Gulf Coast. There are cool cities like New Orleans, weird wildlife, and interesting natural history. Let's look at a few examples from states in this unique part of the United States.

Texas

The strange-looking armadillo is the official state small mammal of Texas.

Legend has it that many Spanish treasure ships wrecked off the coast of South Padre Island, which is part of Texas. To this day, treasure hunters come there to search for gold and silver.

Texas was an independent country from 1836 to 1845 before it became a U.S. state.

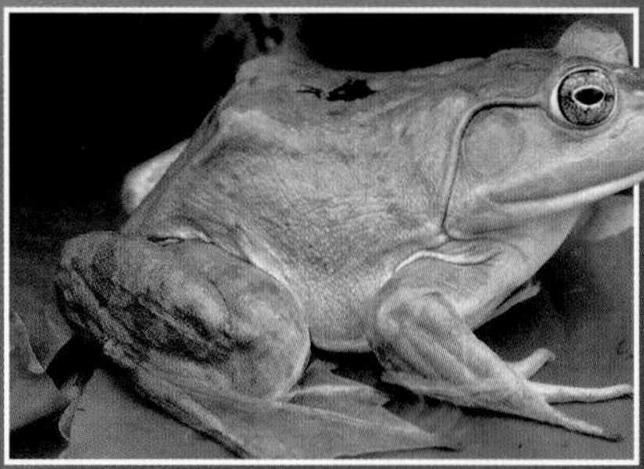

Louisiana

With its many frogs and frog-themed events, the city of Rayne is the world's "Frog Capital"!

The town of Jean Lafitte was a hideout for pirates in the 1800s.

The American Rose Center in Shreveport grows green roses called *Rosa monstrosa*.

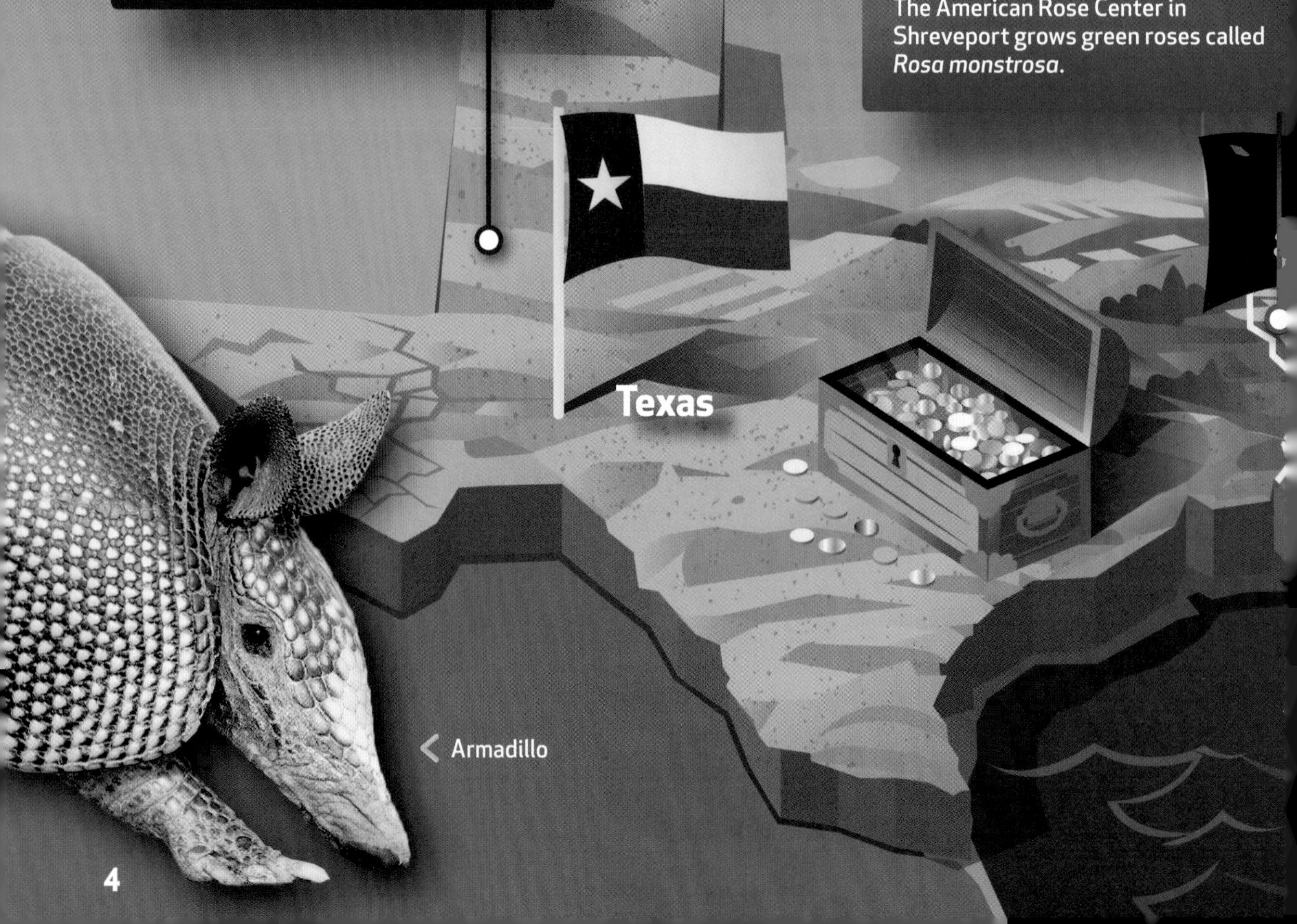

< Armadillo

Mississippi

Gulfport calls itself the "Root Beer Capital of the World," possibly because a famous brand of root beer was started near there.

Visitors to the town of Flora can see petrified trees. An ancient river carried these trees to where they were covered with soil. Over thousands of years the trees turned to stone.

The Teddy bear got its name because President Teddy Roosevelt refused to shoot a bear while hunting in Mississippi.

Alabama

In Magnolia Springs, mail carriers bring the mail by boat.

During flooding, groups of Alabama's fire ants grab onto each other to form a raft so they can float!

Alabama has a giant statue dedicated to an insect—the boll weevil, which destroyed the cotton crop in the early 1900s.

> Flamingo

Florida

Florida's pink flamingos get their unusual color from eating shrimp.

Florida is the only place where alligators and crocodiles live in the same region.

The Seminole Indians of Florida have a word, *Opatishawockalocka* (OP-uh-TISH-uh-WOK-uh-LOK-uh), *that* means "a dry place in the swamp covered with many trees."

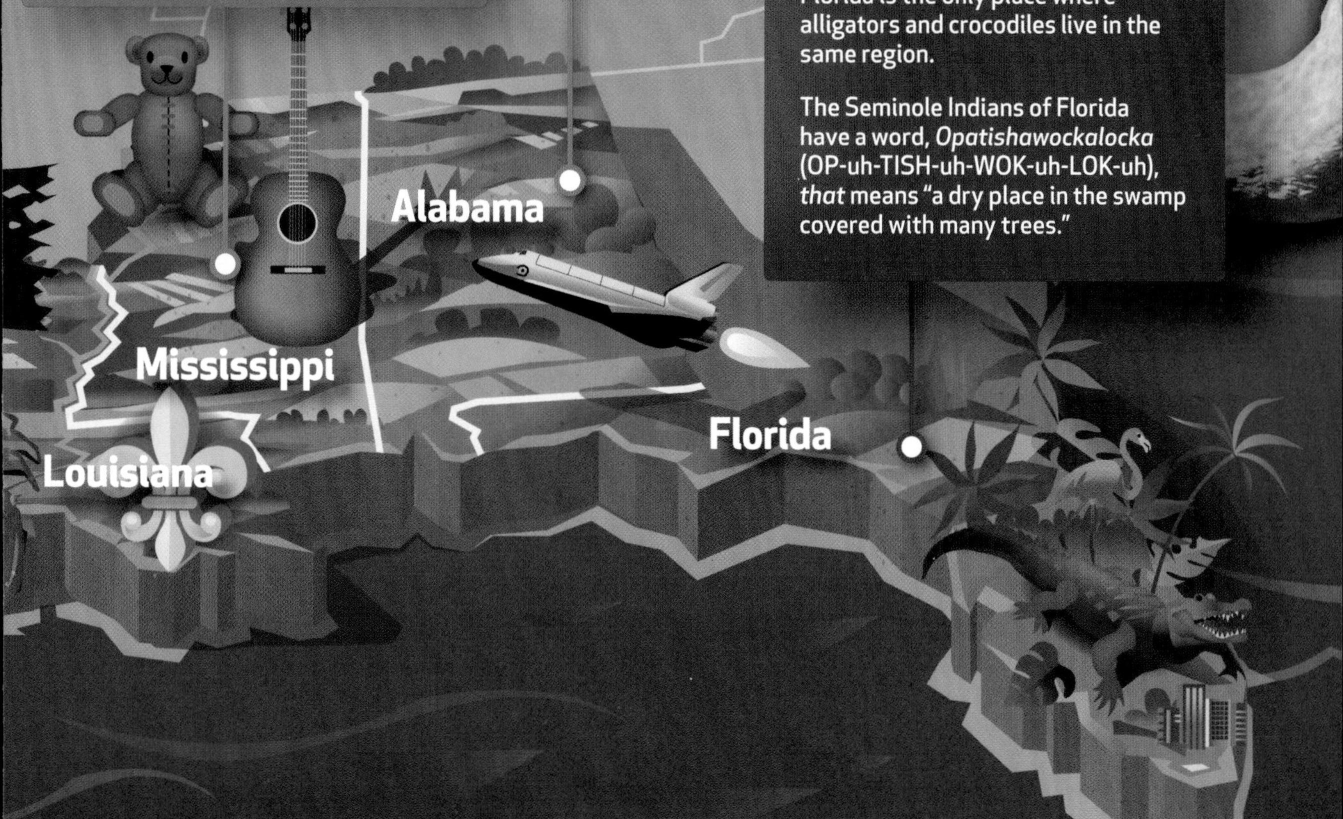

Check In How would you describe the land and water of the Gulf Coast?

GENRE Science Article | **Read to find out** about two amazing creatures of the Gulf Coast region.

Jellies and Other Creatures!

by Grace Coffey

Gaze out over the Gulf of Mexico on a summer night. You might see strange, glowing creatures. They are called jellyfish, but they're not fish, and they're definitely not made of jelly. Jellyfish can be transparent, or see-through, or glow an eerie bright white. They can also be brown, pink, white, or blue. There are 200 different kinds of jellyfish.

Jellyfish have no spines. Between their outer and inner layers of skin is a squishy jelly-like substance that gives the jellyfish its shape—and its name. They float through the water with ocean **currents** and move up and down by opening and closing their bell-shaped bodies. The ocean currents often wash jellyfish up on the beach as the tide comes in.

A jellyfish has no brain. Instead, a system of nerves—fibers in the body that send signals to other parts—helps it detect light, feel the movement of water around it, and smell things. Mostly it uses its **tentacles**, or arms, to pick up tiny **organisms** to eat. But jellyfish also hunt bigger fish. If a fish touches a jellyfish's tentacles, it will get a poisonous sting. The poison stuns the fish, leaving it helpless. Then the jellyfish pulls the fish into its mouth.

Jellyfish live in all the world's salty oceans, usually in coastal waters. Very few have been found in freshwater. Usually jellyfish are tiny, ranging from one inch to just over one foot in length. But some jellies are giants—measuring a whopping seven feet long with frightening tentacles as long as 200 feet!

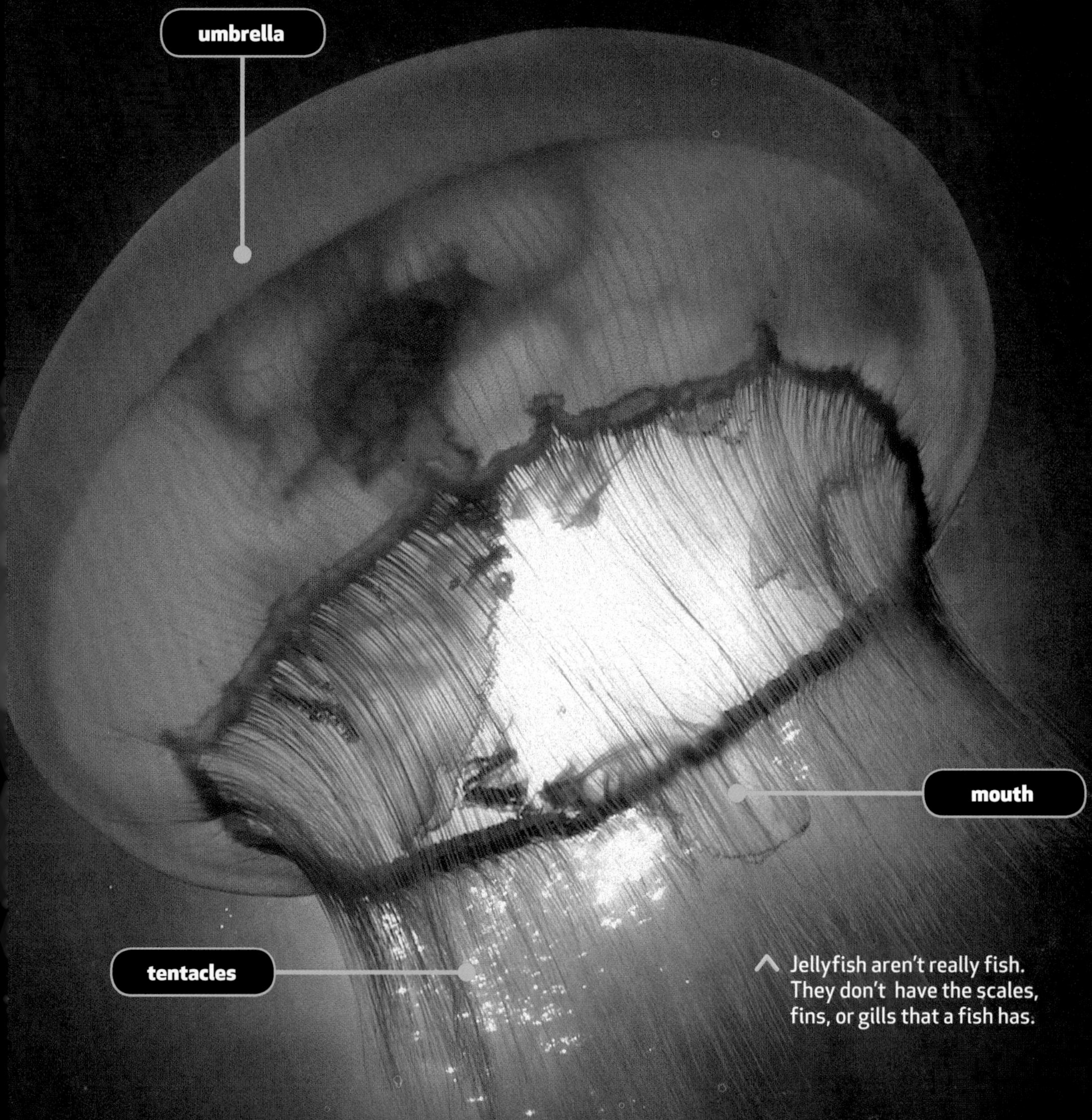

^ Jellyfish aren't really fish. They don't have the scales, fins, or gills that a fish has.

^ One of the Gulf's most common jellyfish is the cannonball jelly. It gets its name from its cannonball-like shape.

Ouch, That Stings!

Watch out! Jellyfish are not aggressive to humans, but they can be hard to see in the water, and you can still get a painful sting if you bump into one accidentally.

A jellyfish's tentacles have tiny stingers in them, like hooks. The stingers contain venom, or poison, that shoots out when the jellyfish touches something. Even after a jellyfish dies, the tentacles remain dangerous. You can get stung by stepping on a dried-out, dead jellyfish on the beach.

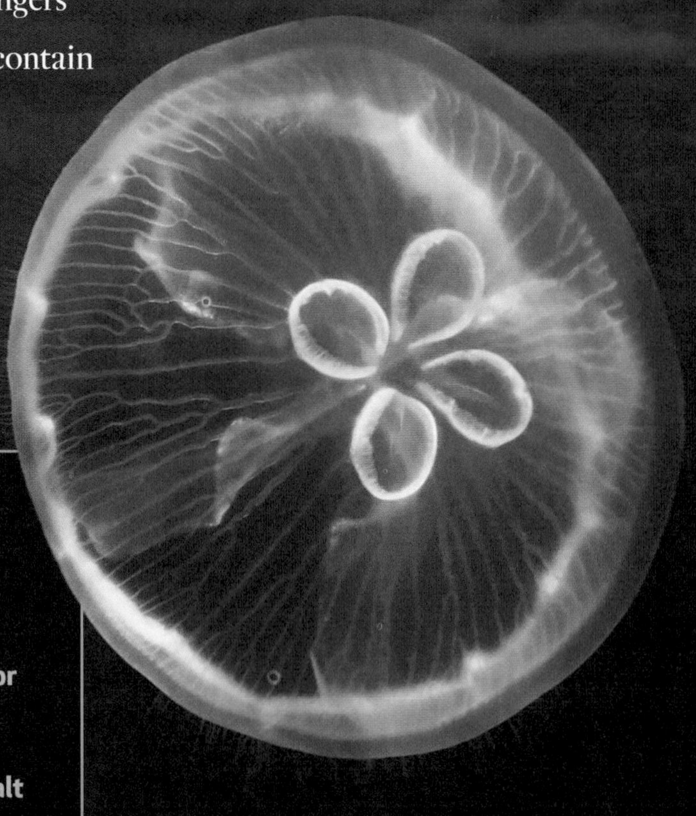

The moon jellyfish is also common in the Gulf. How do you think it got its name?

If you get stung by a jellyfish:

1. Leave the water. Tell a lifeguard or another adult.
2. Rinse the sting with vinegar or salt water. Rinsing can help stop the stinging. Do not use freshwater—that will just increase the stinging feeling.
3. With a stick or towel, scrape off any tentacles that are stuck to your skin.
4. If you have trouble breathing or feel sick or dizzy, get medical help immediately. Do the same if the redness spreads, or if you get bumps.

It LOOKS Like a Jellyfish...

Along Gulf Coast beaches, you'll find another squishy creature, the Portuguese (POR-chuh-geez) man-of-war. It's quite similar to a jellyfish, with a rounded floating top and long poisonous tentacles, but it's also WAY different. It's not even one single creature, but *four* kinds of creatures connected and working together. These strange creatures, called polyps (PAHL-uhps), can look very different.

The polyp at the top gives the man-of-war its name. It floats on the water like a balloon, looking a little bit like an old, wartime sailing ship called a man-of-war. Other polyps make up the poisonous tentacles. The tentacles are usually about 30 feet long, but some can reach as long as 150 feet or more. These deadly arms paralyze or kill prey and carry it to the man-of-war's mouth, where another polyp digests it.

Men-of-war live in oceans around the world. And they live in groups—you may see 1,000 or more floating together.

Portuguese men-of-war are also called bluebottles. The name comes from the blue color of the polyp that floats on the water.

Check In Describe three facts that surprised you about jellyfish or men-of-war.

GENRE Economics Article

Read to find out what kind of work people do on the Gulf Coast.

All in a Day's Work

by Brett Gover

Many people who want to live in a warm place choose the Gulf Coast because of the excellent weather, diverse wildlife, and beautiful beaches. But people who live here have to work, too, and the Gulf Coast has many different jobs to offer.

First, let's look at jobs on the water. People work on the Gulf and on rivers and canals. Ships travel these coastal waterways, delivering goods to the region's many harbors. There are a lot of jobs on these huge ships, as well as on the docks, loading and unloading goods.

How about jobs underneath the water? Workers drill down through deep water to reach oil. We use oil to fuel cars and heat homes. Oil is in other products, too, such as paint and even toothpaste.

Between the surface of the Gulf of Mexico and the oil buried far below its sandy bottom live many millions of fish, and many people work in the fishing industry. Without Gulf Coast seafood, much of the country wouldn't have foods like oysters and shrimp.

Don't forget tourism. Every year, millions of people visit the Gulf Coast to enjoy beaches, underwater marvels, and wildlife tours. That creates jobs for many Gulf Coast residents.

A ranger glides in an airboat through the Everglades. The Everglades is a swamp at the southern tip of Florida. It makes up the eastern edge of the Gulf Coast.

Trawling for Shrimp

Hi! I'm Jackie. Today I'm going out shrimping with my Uncle Mick on his trawler, a boat that drags trawls, or enormous nets, along the seafloor. A large trawler can catch thousands of pounds of shrimp in one day.

5:00 A.M. It's early, but I'm wide awake. As we chug-chug out of the harbor, I help Uncle Mick check the boat's equipment—the ropes, pulleys, anchors, and nets.

6:30 A.M. The sun is up! Uncle Mick hauls up his first catch of shrimp. We pack the squiggly shrimp on ice. They look like huge insects. Uncle Mick points out a quiet, scary shark circling the boat, attracted to our bait.

10:00 A.M. The shark's gone, but storm clouds head in. Storms can churn up waves powerful enough to tip our trawler, so we cruise back to the harbor to wait out the bad weather.

2:00 P.M. We're back on the water after the storm, and Uncle Mick asks me to fix a tear in the netting. I wonder if the shark did this. Repair done!

4:00 P.M. We haul up the last catch. We've caught lots of shrimp today, so we head to port, where we'll sell the catch. Then we go home for dinner. After seeing shrimp all day, we're ready for cheeseburgers.

Smaller shrimp boats like this one are best for fishing in shallow water.

These workers are drilling for oil on a rig. Workers on a rig need to wear helmets and goggles when doing this dangerous job.

Drilling for Oil on the Seafloor

I'm Jerry, an oil worker on a Gulf rig. A rig is a platform in the ocean where oil is gathered from beneath the seafloor. Since the rig is so far out to sea, we stay here and work for weeks at a time. A large rig is like a little city, with a cafeteria, a theater, a gym, and a store—not that we get too much free time. The pay is good, but the work is hard and dangerous, and we work 12-hour shifts.

6:00 A.M. It's meeting time, and managers discuss two important things—keeping oil flowing and keeping workers safe. Oil from one rig might bring in more than a billion dollars a year, so we can't let the oil stop flowing. The worst thing that can happen is an oil spill—it hurts the environment, wastes oil, and costs money. As one of the drillers, I work with a team to make sure that doesn't happen, but it's always a danger with the complex machinery we use.

7:00 A.M. to 7:00 P.M. We start by checking our instruments, making repairs, and moving equipment into place. The danger of explosions is on our minds as we handle monster-sized machinery. The oil comes up through pipes and goes to a tank. Then workers pump it into a ship, which takes it to be processed. The rig operates all day long. When we sign off at 7:00 P.M., new workers sign on. After dinner, I'll call my family and then I'll hit the bunk room with a book.

Many trainers have studied biology and animal behavior.

Training Dolphins

I'm Morgan, a dolphin trainer at a Gulf Coast marine park. Some people think dolphins shouldn't be used for entertainment. Lots of groups rescue sick or injured dolphins, nurse them to health, and release them. But most dolphins in parks such as ours were born here. Trainers work to keep the dolphins in these parks healthy and happy.

6:30 A.M. to Noon I'm on the first shift, so I "bucket it out" for the morning meal. A dolphin gobbles as many as 20 pounds of fish a day or more! I swim with the dolphins and keep them moving and learning with hand signals, whistles, and treats. My favorite dolphin, Tansy, nudges me affectionately. Whenever a dolphin does something cool, I throw it a fish. That's an effective training technique for these highly intelligent mammals.

1:00 P.M. After noontime feeding comes the day's highlight—the dolphin show! I feel the crowd's excitement. The dolphins love to show the audience how smart they are. I give a hand signal, and two dolphins swim, jump and flip together, and land with a splash. People near the water get wet, but they don't mind.

3:00 P.M. Show's over, and so is my shift, but I sit and take notes on what I've learned. I note the dolphins' moods, new noises, appearance, and anything else I remember. I talk to our scientists and doctors about the dolphins. I'm lucky to have such a close relationship with these marine mammals. Working with them every day is fun.

Check In What kinds of jobs do people have in the Gulf Coast region?

GENRE **Opinion Piece**

Read to find out about how oil is used and the pros and cons of drilling for oil.

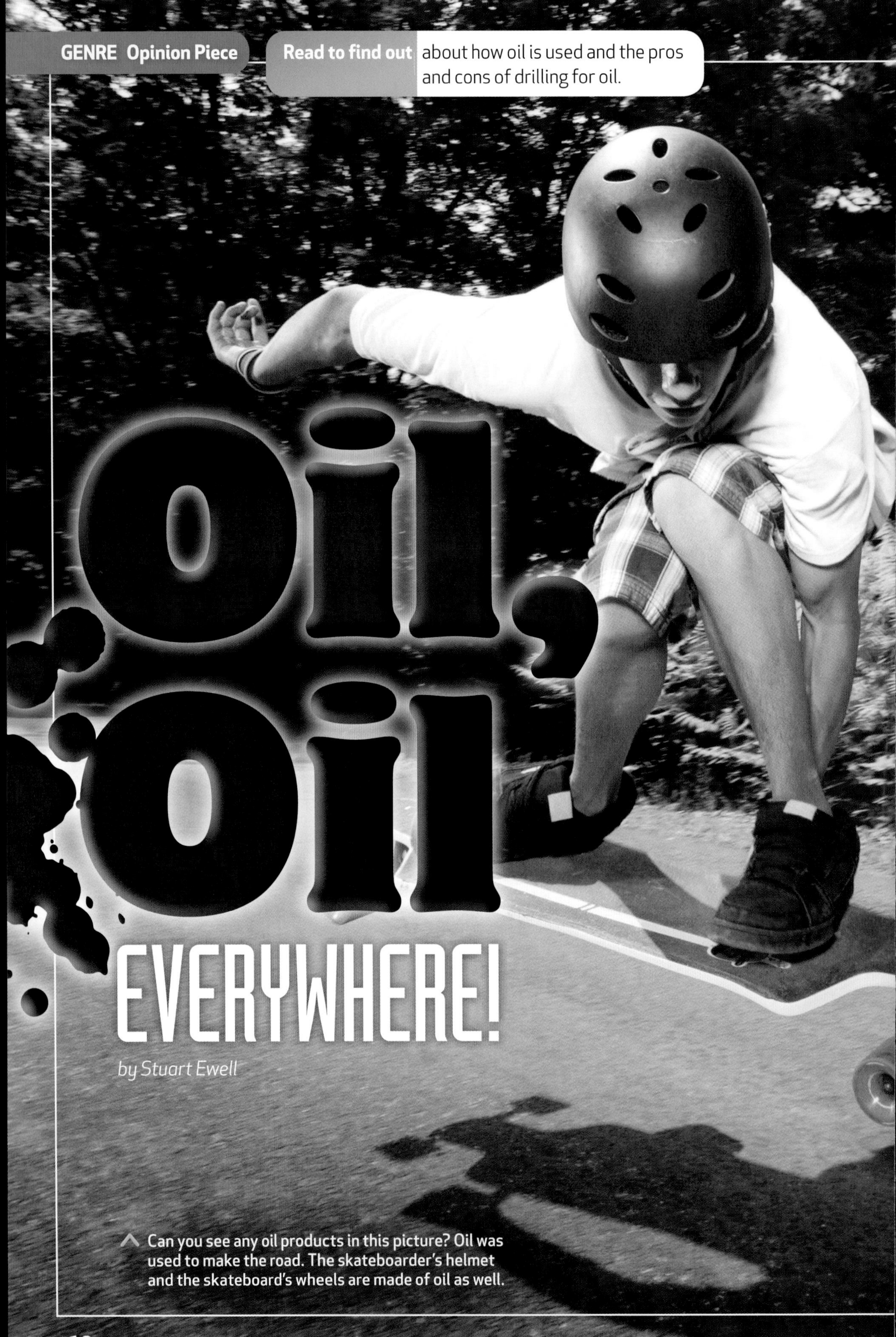

Oil, Oil EVERYWHERE!

by Stuart Ewell

Can you see any oil products in this picture? Oil was used to make the road. The skateboarder's helmet and the skateboard's wheels are made of oil as well.

Oil as a fuel is very important. Oil and the products that come from it help us heat our homes and power our cars. It's also used to make many of the products we use every day. From cameras to tennis rackets, and even hair coloring, oil is a very useful substance. But sometimes oil can create problems. It can **pollute**, or poison, the land and the water where many plants and animals live. Burning oil as a fuel can harm the atmosphere, which is the blanket of air that covers Earth.

Oil is found deep beneath the ground. It collects in large pools, called **reserves**, all over the world, including under the Gulf of Mexico. Maybe you've seen cartoons that show characters digging into the ground until black liquid suddenly shoots into the sky. They make finding and collecting oil look easy, but we know it's not that simple.

1. Hundreds of millions of years ago, tiny bits of dead plants and animals (shown in brown and green above) were buried beneath mud (gray). Some bits were buried under the ocean (blue), some were not.
2. Over time, heat and pressure turned some of the mud into heavy rock. This rock layer (dark brown) pressed down on the layer of dead plants and animals.
3. The immense pressure turned the plants and animals into oil (black) and other fuels we collect from below the ocean's floor today.

M.U. 726-A
OCS-G-20605

Drilling in the Sea

Think of how you use a straw to drink a glass of orange juice. To pull the juice into our mouths, we add suction, or pressure, on the straw. We get oil from underground in a similar way. Oil drillers use an engine to create the pressure needed to suck the oil up a pipe to Earth's surface.

The easiest way to get oil is to dig in the ground, so that's where companies began looking for oil reserves. Now that people have been collecting oil for more than 150 years, the oil under land is harder to find. Scientists have started looking under the ocean floor for oil.

Oil companies use structures called **derricks** to extract oil from under the sea. A derrick looks like a tower on a platform. Derricks are built above the place on the ocean floor where oil has been found. Pulleys and cables attached to the derrick move huge drills up and down into the hole in the ocean floor. Then pumps and pipes carry the oil up to the derrick, where it is placed in tanks.

This huge oil rig is located along the Gulf Coast. It is near Port Aransas, Texas.

PRO: It Makes Our World Run

There are obvious uses for oil. The two main reasons we use oil are to fuel our cars and heat our homes. But we need oil for many other things. We use oil to make electricity. It powers the refrigerators we use to keep our food cold and the ovens we use for cooking. Oil also powers the pump that brings water to our houses and the machine that heats our water.

Plastic building blocks are made from oil products.

Want to wash your hair or play outside? Your shampoo, your playground equipment, and your soccer ball might all have been made with oil products. Anything plastic has oil in it. Even the soles of your shoes may be made from oil.

Think of how long it would take to walk the distance a car, train, or plane can travel in just one hour. Imagine the number of people it would take to dig the foundation of a building or to pave an interstate highway without modern machinery that runs on fuel made from oil.

Oil products are very useful. We count on them every day. We are **dependent** on them. The more items we use that are made from oil, the more oil we need to find. So, oil drilling is necessary until we can learn to use less of it, or find other fuel options.

Gas made from oil powers lawn mowers. Their tires are also made from oil products.

Industrial oil is used to make gasoline.

Most basketballs are made with oil.

People use oil to build the parts of a car. Oil powers cars, too.

CON: Stop the Drilling!

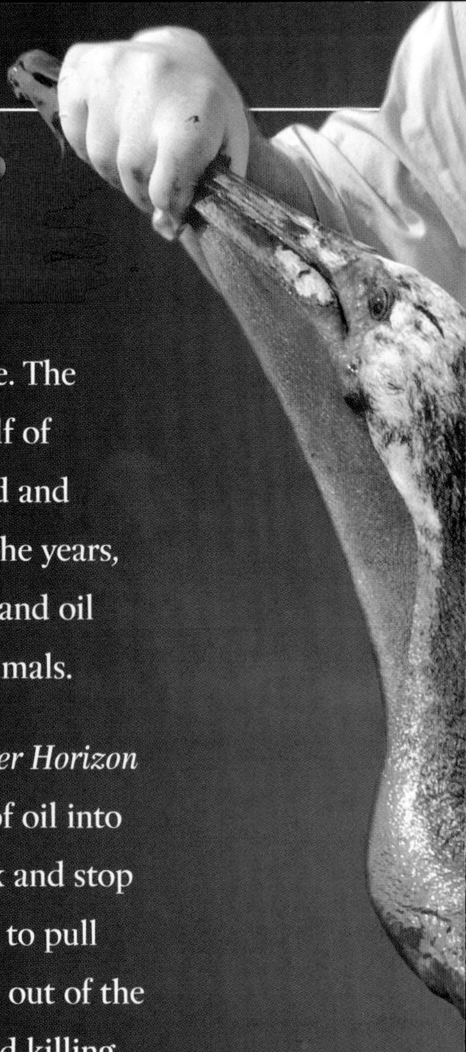

While oil is very useful, drilling for oil has its downside. The dangers of drilling for oil in the deep waters of the Gulf of Mexico are many, and workers have to be highly skilled and follow safety rules to prevent accidents. Even so, over the years, explosions on oil rigs have injured and killed workers, and oil spills have polluted our waters and killed countless animals.

In April 2010, an explosion on the oil derrick *Deepwater Horizon* took 11 human lives and spilled thousands of gallons of oil into the Gulf of Mexico. It took five months to seal the leak and stop the flow of oil into the Gulf. Chemicals had to be used to pull the oil out of the water. The oil that couldn't be pulled out of the ocean eventually washed up onto beaches, covering and killing plants and animals. The Gulf is still recovering from that disaster.

The oil spill affected the Gulf in many ways. Many fish died, which hurt the environment, as well as the fishing economy. Tourism also went down. Fewer people visited, because people can't sunbathe on oil-covered beaches or swim in dirty water. When people didn't come, restaurants and hotels had to close. Many people lost their jobs because of the spill.

Oil makes people's lives better in many ways, but drilling for oil can also make life in a region worse. True, we do need oil. But we don't want oil to continue to pollute our waters and destroy habitats, or places where plants and animals live. We use so much of it, but as oil becomes harder to find, we will have to find other sources of power to run our world. Let's start now.

When oil spills, volunteers help clean up by shoveling oily sand off beaches. Workers clean the feathers of birds in this picture. The birds have been coated in oil from the Gulf oil spill.

Check In What are some products in your home that are made with oil?

GENRE Narrative

Read to find out about one of the biggest hurricanes to hit the Gulf Coast.

Deadly Winds

by Elizabeth Massie

^ This painting is an artist's depiction of the destruction Galveston suffered during the 1900 hurricane.

Violent winds scream, driving rain slams to the ground, trees fall, buildings cave in, monster waves crash onto land, and water rises. What's happening? It's a **hurricane**.

There are lots of storms in the Gulf Coast region. The Gulf's warm, moist air collides with dry, cooler air blowing down from the north. The warm water whips the cooler air into strong winds. As the winds blow faster, they can spin into a hurricane. Over the years, many serious hurricanes have pounded the Gulf Coast region.

One of the most destructive hurricanes ever to strike the United States changed Galveston, Texas, forever. This busy, island city on the Gulf Coast was home to more than 35,000 people. On September 8, 1900, about 6,000 people died in the hurricane and the city was heavily damaged.

Days before the storm hit, the Weather Bureau in Washington, D.C., warned Galveston that a storm was crossing the Gulf and heading toward the city. But in those days, forecasters couldn't tell how powerful a storm would be or exactly where it would hit.

This map shows the path the hurricane of 1900 took.

Storm warning flags went up in the harbor telling people to stay out of the water. But locals had lived through many storms before and weren't afraid. When the hurricane struck, the powerful wind and waves knocked down electrical wires and caused rapid flooding. The director of the Galveston Weather Office later wrote:

> **I reached home and found the water around my residence waist deep. I at once went to work assisting people . . . into my residence. . . . By 8 p.m. a number of houses had drifted up and lodged to the east and southeast of my residence, and these with the force of the waves acted as a battering ram . . . and at 8:30 p.m. my residence went down with about fifty persons who had sought it for safety.**

The Deadly Storm Strikes

Violent winds pushed water over the island throughout the day and into the night. Some buildings were torn apart and others were flattened. **Debris**, or scattered remains of objects or buildings, filled the area.

Milton Elford lived in Galveston. During the storm, his family and neighbors left their homes and hurried to a larger house nearby. They hoped the house would withstand the storm, but it didn't. Milton survived but his family did not. Later, he wrote:

> **We all gathered in one room; all at once the house went from its foundation and the water came in waist-deep, and we all made a break for the door, but could not get it open. We then smashed out the window and I led the way. I had only got part way out when the house fell on us. I was hit on the head with something and it knocked me out and into the water head first. . . . I came up and got hold of some wreckage on the other side of the house.**

Samuel Young watched the storm first from the beach and then the wharf, or place along the water's edge where ships land. Finally, he went home and described what he saw from his window:

> **The debris fairly flew past, so rapid had the tide become. At twenty minutes to six o'clock . . . there was a marked increase in the violence of the wind. . . . I saw the tide rise fully four feet in one bound. In a few minutes several houses . . . went to pieces and floated away.**

At first, Galveston resident Ida Smith Austin wasn't too concerned about the approaching storm, but her opinion soon changed:

> **The wind seemed to grow more furious reaching the incredible velocity [force] of 120 miles an hour. Blinds were torn off windows, frames, sash and all, blown in, and the rainwater stood an inch and a half on upstairs floors.**

The Galveston hurricane destroyed more than 2,500 homes. Buildings were knocked down by strong winds and pounding waves. The water rose as high as 15 to 20 feet.

Many houses along the Gulf Coast are built on stilts. This one is boarded up as Hurricane Ike approaches.

After the Storm

After the storm, people across America wanted to help the survivors of Galveston. Some sent money, while others traveled there to lend a hand cleaning up and repairing the city. Clara Barton, the founder of the Red Cross, arrived on September 17, 1900. She brought workers who gave out food and clothes to the survivors.

To protect the city from future storms, engineers designed a 17-foot-high seawall, a wall that stops the waves from hitting the shore. That seawall still stands today. They also raised the island's land to make it higher in some areas. These improvements helped when Hurricane Ike hit the island, over 100 years later, in 2008. Though that hurricane **devastated** Galveston, early warnings allowed many people to leave the city before it hit. It is estimated that 74 people died in Hurricane Ike, compared with the thousands who died in 1900.

Hurricanes cannot be stopped, but with modern technology, meteorologists can keep an eye on them. The National Hurricane Center uses airplanes and satellites to track the progress and power of hurricanes. The planes and satellites allow them to predict dangerous storms earlier. Then people in the storm's path can be warned to leave the area before the deadly winds strike.

Check In How did the people of Galveston make it a safer city after the hurricane?

Discuss

1. What connections can you make among the five selections in this book? How are the selections related?

2. How are people who live on the Gulf Coast affected by the water and land around them?

3. What are the advantages and disadvantages of drilling for oil in the Gulf?

4. Compare the hurricanes that hit Galveston in 1900 and 2008. How did changes in weather forecasting technology affect how people weathered each storm?

5. What do you still wonder about the Gulf Coast? How can you learn more?